CONTENTS

Recreation Leader

Hero Hotline:

Called Together to Serve God!

	Bible Story	Hotline Tips	Music	Crafts
Session 1	Jesus Builds the Team John 1:35-51	Heroes are called to... Follow Jesus!	• Hero Hotline Theme Song • If U Wanna Be A Hero	• Hotline Comics • Hotline Cuff
Session 2	Shiphrah, Puah, and Miriam: God's Wonder Women Exodus 1:8–2:10	Heroes are called to... Help Others!	• Hold Up • Beat Like Yours	• Helping Hero Medal • Basket of Blessings
Session 3	Jethro Mentors Moses Exodus 18	Heroes are called to... Work Together!	• Let's Strive • Work Together	• Hero Puppet Team • Work Together Painting
Session 4	The Magnificent Magi Matthew 2:1-12	Heroes are called to... Listen to God!	• Good Good Life • Show Grace, Speak Truth	• Magi's Guiding Star • Hero Shield • Stars and Straws
Session 5	Unexpected Heroes Give Paul a Basket Ride Acts 9:1-25	Heroes are called to... Show Grace!	• Your Grace • That's What Makes A Hero	• Hero Team Frame

Hero Verse

So let's strive for the things that bring peace and the things that build each other up. (Romans 14:19)

Science	Recreation	Snacks	Notes
• Magnetic Attraction • Sinking Soda	• Hero Quick-Change • Heroic Catch • Hero Headquarters • Preschool Recreation	• Build Your Own Fig Tree • Super Vision Sticks • Nathanael's Fig Tree Fruit Bars	
• Bubbling Up • Super Straw	• Hero Helping Toss • Don't Wake the Baby • Practice Makes Heroes • Preschool Recreation	• Hope Heroes • Pretzel Power Lifts • Banana Boats	
• Power Paper • Super Bubble Blower	• Work Together Tag • Find the Team • Quickening Questions • Preschool Recreation	• Healthy Campfire • Campfire Trail Mix • Work Together Pizza	
• The Leak-Proof Bag • Looking for the Star	• Guided by a Star • Return Home Another Way • Heroic Attention • Preschool Recreation	• Colossal Courage Cookies • Veggie Treasures • Hero Ropes	
• Flying Ping-Pong Ball • Incredible Ice • Bonus Experiment: Liquid Light	• Grace Tag • Team Up! • Build a Basket • Preschool Recreation	• Marvelous Mini Cakes • Cones of Power • Basket Snacks	

Equipping Your Recreation Station

Tips for Leaders!

- Attend all Hero Hotline leader training sessions to discover how your station fits into the overall message of the program.
- Work with your Director to recruit a team of amazing volunteers who will assist you, monitor safety, and turn to God to meet our needs.
- Collect all materials for each session well in advance. Get your congregation involved by publicizing a list of supplies they can donate!
- Take time to read through the lessons and practice the games in advance with your volunteers.
- Review the "Object" and "Preparation" for each game with your leadership team before each session begins. Make time to use the "Bible Tie-in" with each group before they depart for their next activity.
- Remember that materials for the activities can be adapted to fit your church's needs and budgets. For example, if someone in your group has a latex allergy, substitute foam balls in place of balloons. Be creative in using what you already have on hand.
- Please note the heading of each session's games for Intensity Level expectations. Preschool/ Kindergarten-appropriate options are on pages 9, 13, 17, 21, and 25.
- Feel free to adapt any of the games and activities as best fits your groups, space, and time allotment. We know that every church and program is unique, so make each session your own, and have fun with it!
- Check out the FREE "Guidelines for Buddies of Special Needs Heroes" at CokesburyVBS.com for ideas on how to help all Heroes participate at their level of comfort and ability.
- **SAFETY TIP!** Check your surroundings before each session by making sure the areas are free of breakable objects and trip or fall hazards that could endanger Heroes while they are in your care.

Working Together to Bring Peace

Hero Hotline VBS is based on Romans 14:19 (CEB): “So let’s strive for the things that bring peace and the things that build each other up.” This verse reminds us that God calls us to be a part of a community—working to bring peace to the world is something that we are all called to do together.

Here’s how Hero Hotline helps Heroes work together to bring peace and build one another up:

The Hero Hotline Headquarters is a secret place where Heroes go to help solve problems called in by other heroes out in the community. At Hero Hotline, everyone’s gifts are valued and each hero has a role to play. Heroes receive a call/assignment each day by the Professor and Super Meer to help solve a problem that other Heroes in the community are facing. Heroes will then explore the files and database of the Hero Hotline to discover how heroes can work together to bring peace.

Peace comes from God, and as God’s people we are called to share that peace with the world. We work together, help each other, and encourage each other because God has called us to live in community and fellowship with one another. We all can strive, in both expected and unexpected ways, to bring peace, love and justice to the world.

Here’s how each session will highlight the ways we can work together as a team to strive for peace and build each other up:

- By recognizing that we are all a part of the family of God by our faith in Jesus. Just as the disciples were called to follow Jesus, we are also called to follow and be a part of his team.

- By recognizing that our faith in God calls us to help others in need and stand up for what is right. Just like Shiphrah, Puah, and Miriam stood up against the injustices of the Pharaoh, we can speak up for those who need help.

- By learning that Heroes can’t go at it alone! Just like Moses took his father-in-law’s advice to build a team of people to help share the load, we too can look to mentors and friends to work alongside us to do what God has called us to do.

- By discovering that God speaks to and directs us in many ways. Just like the magi were directed by a star and a dream, we can receive Gods words and direction when we pay attention to the Bible, creation, the people God puts in our lives, and so many other ways.

- By finding ways to show grace to others. Paul’s story began with grace being offered to him, both from Jesus and from some of the other disciples. People who once didn’t like Paul helped him to safety! We too can offer grace to those around us.

Bible Story

Jesus Builds the Team
John 1:35-51

Hotline Verse

So let's strive for the things that bring peace and the things that build each other up.
(Romans 14:19)

Hotline Tip

Heroes are called to…
Follow Jesus!

Materials

(one set for each team)

- basket/container
- cape
- headband
- hero cuffs
- hero shield
- mask
- any other hero costume items that might appeal to your particular group

(for the playing area)

- cones or masking tape

Test Church Tip

- Have younger groups put on only one or two costume pieces, or have them seek assistance from helpers.

High Intensity:

Hero Quick-Change

Object

Heroes will reinforce the Hero Hotline theme and first Hotline Tip through a relay race.

Preparation

Make sure the recreation area is safe and ready for play. Use cones or tape to mark a starting line and a finish line. Separate items for each team into different baskets, and place the baskets behind the starting line.

Let's Play!

Many people love heroes and their stories so much, they even dress up as their favorites for birthday parties or other special events. In this game, we are going to practice dressing up as heroes in a race against time and each other!

1. Divide your group into teams, and ask each team to line up behind the starting line.

2. When you instruct the Heroes to begin, the first person on each team must put on all of the costume pieces. Then, that person carries the basket to the finish line, removes the costume pieces, puts them back in the basket, and runs while carrying the basket back to the starting line. If any items are dropped in the process, that Hero must retrieve them before continuing.

3. Upon returning to the starting line, the Hero hands the basket of costume items to the next player, who must repeat the process.

4. Play continues until all Heroes have completed the relay.

Bible Tie-ins

It sure is fun to dress up like a hero, isn't it? What would your own hero costume look like?

The Bible has many stories of great heroes—including the disciples from our first story. But God's heroes don't have costumes. In fact, you can't tell who is a hero for God just by looking at a person. God's heroes are known for their actions of following Jesus. Jesus chose the disciples to help him do his heroic work in the world. Working together as a team is what made them heroes.

How can you be a hero like the disciples, even without a fancy costume?

Let's say our first Hotline Tip together. (*Say the tip in unison.*) **Heroes are called to follow Jesus!**

Medium Intensity:

Heroic Catch

Object

Heroes will memorize or reinforce the Hotline Verse through an increasingly challenging game of passing and catching a set of playground balls.

Preparation

Make sure the recreation area is safe and ready for play. Secure headbands around playground balls to differentiate the balls from one another (or use playground balls that are different colors).

Let's Play!

We're going to need our Hotline Verse to help us in this game. Let's say the Hotline Verse together: "So let's strive for the things that bring peace and the things that build each other up." Romans 14:19

Great! Now the key to this activity is paying attention. You have to be on the lookout for which ball is coming your direction at *all* times. Ready?

1. Ask your Heroes to form a large circle with several feet between each person.

2. Choose one ball and pass it around the circle clockwise. Each Hero should say, "So let's strive" to the person to the left as the ball is passed. Practice this pattern once around the circle.

3. Set the first ball aside. Choose a second ball and pass it around the circle counterclockwise. Heroes should say "for the things that bring peace" to their right-hand neighbors as they pass the ball. Practice this pattern once around the circle.

4. Set the second ball aside. The last ball must be bounced to someone across the circle. Heroes will call out the name of their chosen person, followed by "and the things that build each other up." Practice this a few times.

5. Add the first ball back into the circle, so that the "So let's strive" ball is traveling clockwise and the "and the things that build each other up" ball is being bounced across the circle.

6. Add the "for the things that bring peace" ball into the circle, so that all three are in active rotation. See how quickly the balls can travel around the circle without any mistakes!

Bible Tie-in

Was one ball or direction more difficult for you than the others? If so, why do you think that is?

Do you think you could have handled it with even more balls added into the mix?

There are *way* more than three distractions coming at us every day, yet Jesus wants us to focus on and follow him. Be on the lookout for every opportunity to be a hero to others by following Jesus' teachings, and don't accidentally "catch" a distraction!

Bible Story

Jesus Builds the Team
John 1:35-51

Hotline Verse

So let's strive for the things that bring peace and the things that build each other up.
(Romans 14:19)

Hotline Tip

Heroes are called to…
Follow Jesus!

Materials

- three medium-size plastic or rubber playground balls plus three elastic headbands (red, yellow, and blue) **OR**
- three medium-size playground balls in different colors or with different hero logos/images

Teacher Tip

- Ribbon, colored duct tape, or painter's tape could take the place of the headbands.

Bible Story

Jesus Builds the Team
John 1:35-51

Hotline Verse

So let's strive for the things that bring peace and the things that build each other up.
(Romans 14:19)

Hotline Tip

Heroes are called to…
Follow Jesus!

Materials

- newspapers and/or food boxes (cereal, crackers, etc.), cut along one seam and laid flat
- large empty cardboard boxes
- masking tape
- heavy objects such as hardback books
- optional: rulers

Low Intensity:

Hero Headquarters

Object

Heroes will reinforce the Bible story while working in teams to build their own Hero Headquarters location.

Preparation

1. Make sure the recreation area is safe and ready for play.
2. Organize newspapers and/or boxes and masking tape into stacks for teams.
3. Have some hardback books or other weighty objects on hand to use as stabilizers, when needed.

Optional: Provide rulers for teams to measure the height of their buildings.

Let's Play!

SAY SOMETHING LIKE: **At Hero Hotline, we are learning how to work together as a team of heroes that brings peace and builds each other up, and most importantly follows Jesus. In our first Bible story, Jesus puts together a team of heroes for exactly this purpose.**

Lots of heroes from comic books or movies and TV have a hero headquarters where they meet to work together. It could be a cave, like at Hero Hotline, or another type of meeting place. Today, we are going work in teams to design a model for our own Hero Headquarters.

1. Divide Heroes into teams of three or four.

2. Encourage teams to work together to build a Hero Headquarters. Consider even designating a height requirement for the structures (at least twelve inches tall, for example). Give minimal instructions, allowing Heroes to solve the problem creatively.

3. Decide in advance how much time you'll give the teams to make their headquarters. (Ten minutes is an appropriate amount of time for them to build.)

Bible Tie-in

ASK: **What did you think was the most challenging part of this activity?**

Would it have been easier or harder if you'd had to do it alone, with no teammates?

SAY SOMETHING LIKE:
Your Hero Headquarters look great! They are all great examples of the amazing things we can do when we work together!

Preschool Recreation

Hero Freeze

Preparation

Make sure the recreation area is safe and ready for play. Cue up CD or music tracks and player.

Let's Play!

SAY: **Today we are going to have fun listening to music and moving around.**

When the music stops, I will say our Hotline Verse, "So let's strive for the things that bring peace and the things that build each other up" (Romans 14:19). You can say it with me. When the music starts again, start singing and moving.

1. Play the music and encourage the Heroes to move around and have fun.
2. When the music stops, all moving stops and Heroes freeze in place. Encourage them to freeze in a hero pose.
3. Encourage them to say with you: **"So let's strive for the things that bring peace and the things that build each other up" (Romans 14:19)**
4. Play the music again. Play as long as there is interest.

Bible Tie-in

When you are finished, congratulate the children on being such good Heroes.

SAY: **Heroes are called to follow Jesus. One way we follow Jesus is by learning Bible verses.**

Bring a Friend

Preparation

Make sure the recreation area is safe and ready for play.

Let's Play!

SAY: **When we are followers of Jesus, it's fun to tell our friends about Jesus and invite them to church. Let's pretend to bring our friends to see Jesus.**

1. Have the Heroes choose a friend and go to one side of the room. If you have an uneven number of Heroes, let the children make a group of three.
2. Sit on the opposite side of the room from the Heroes. Hold up the picture of Jesus. Give the Heroes directions on how to move with their friends across the room to you.

   Friend (child's name) **and friend** (child's name)**, hold hands and hop to see Jesus.**
3. Continue the game with other steps like tip-toeing, walking backward, galloping, baby steps, giant steps, and so forth.

Bible Tie-in

When you are finished, congratulate the children on being such good Heroes.

SAY: **Heroes are called to follow Jesus. One way we follow Jesus is by inviting others to "come and see." We can invite our friends to follow Jesus.**

Bible Story

Jesus Builds the Team
John 1:35-51

Hotline Verse

So let's strive for the things that bring peace and the things that build each other up.
(Romans 14:19)

Hotline Tip

Heroes are called to… Follow Jesus!

Materials

Hero Freeze

- **Hero Hotline Complete Music CD**
- CD player

Bring a Friend

- picture of Jesus template

Bible Story

Shiphrah, Puah, and Miriam: God's Wonder Women

Exodus 1:8–2:10

Hotline Verse

So let's strive for the things that bring peace and the things that build each other up. (Romans 14:19)

Hotline Tip

Heroes are called to… Help Others!

Materials

(one set for each team)

- large bucket
- one table tennis ball
- one tennis ball
- one volleyball
- one basketball
- one football
- one baseball
- one soccer ball
- one wiffle ball
- eight labels

(for the playing area)

- cones or masking tape
- paper and tape to label
- buckets
- marker

High Intensity:

Hero Helping Toss

Object

Heroes will reinforce the Hotline Verse by playing a ball toss game.

Preparation

Make sure the recreation area is safe and ready for play. Use cones or masking tape to mark a throwing line. Place large buckets about fifteen feet away from the throwing line.

Label each ball in the set with a keyword from the Hotline Verse (Strive, Bring, Peace, Build, Each, Other, Up, Romans 14:19). Label the large buckets "Hero Helping Power." You will need a complete verse and a bucket for each team.

Let's Play!

You all remember our Hotline Verse, don't you? Let's repeat the Hotline Verse together. *(Say the verse in unison.)* **So let's strive for the things that bring peace and the things that build each other up. Romans 14:19**

Excellent! We're going to use our Hotline Verse today in a friendly ball toss competition.

1. Divide the Heroes into teams, depending on the size of your group. Have each team line up at the throwing line, about fifteen feet from their team's hero helping power bucket.
2. Give each team a set of balls labeled with words from the Hotline Verse. They will need to throw the balls—in order—and sink them into their buckets.
3. The first player from each team tosses the "Strive" ball, trying to sink it into the bucket. If the ball goes in, move to the next player. If it misses, the player must retrieve the ball and try again. After three tries, move to the next player, and so on until that ball goes in.
4. Once the "Strive" ball goes in, the next player attempts to sink the "Bring" ball, and so on.
5. Play continues until one team has gotten all the balls into their bucket.

Bible Tie-in

Shiphrah, Puah, and Miriam were God's wonder women because they helped others. Do you think it was hard or scary for them to live out the Hotline Verse—strive for the things that bring peace and build each other up? Why or why not?

Remember, helping others is an important part of being a hero. This can sometimes be scary or hard, but working together makes it easier!

Medium Intensity:
Don't Wake the Baby

Object
Heroes reinforce the Bible story while participating in a bucket relay race.

Preparation
Make sure the recreation area is safe and ready for play. Use cones or masking tape to mark a goal line for each team. Tie a bell to each basket. Give each team a baby doll and a basket.

Let's Play!
Miriam (and her mother) made the hard decision to help her baby brother Moses by finding someone outside the Hebrew community to keep him safe. Today, we're going to play a game to remind us of the story of baby Moses in his basket.

1. Divide Heroes into two even teams. Teams form two lines facing each other and stretched out across the play area with several steps between each person. (The starting line is at one end of the lines of players and the goal line is at the other end of the lines.)

2. Explain: Each team represents the Nile River. Each team's goal is to help "float" the sleeping baby Moses doll along the Nile without "waking him." Have the first person in line place the baby in the basket. Starting with the first person in line, each player will move quickly but smoothly (so as not to wake the baby) to the next player and pass the baby in the basket to her/him and so on. If a player causes the bell to ring, the baby is "awake" and the player must go to the end of the line. The team must then start passing the baby all over again. (The line will need to shift their spacing to accommodate the person being added to the end.) If everyone in the line is successful at not ringing the bell, the last player will take the baby to the goal line.

Optional: Add fun by allowing the opposing teams to yell "Awake!" if they hear the other team's bell ring. However, they must do so without causing their own bell to ring.

3. The team that successfully passes the basket down their line and makes it to the goal line without ringing the bell wins.

4. Signal the teams to begin and monitor for the bells ringing as they play. Replay the game as many times as desired.

Bible Tie-in
Sometimes God's heroes are called to do difficult things to help others. In our Bible story, Shiphrah, Puah, and Miriam knew that helping Hebrew women and baby boys was the right thing to do, so they helped even when it was hard and against what Pharaoh wanted.

Have you ever had to do something difficult to help someone? With God's help we can do hard things!

Bible Story
Shiphrah, Puah, and Miriam: God's Wonder Women
Exodus 1:8–2:10

Hotline Verse
So let's strive for the things that bring peace and the things that build each other up.
(Romans 14:19)

Hotline Tip
Heroes are called to… Help Others!

Materials
- cones or masking tape
- two baskets
- two bells
- two baby dolls

Bible Story
Shiphrah, Puah, and Miriam: God's Wonder Women
Exodus 1:8–2:10

Hotline Verse
So let's strive for the things that bring peace and the things that build each other up.
(Romans 14:19)

Hotline Tip
Heroes are called to... Help Others!

Materials
- note cards
- pen or pencil
- timer or stopwatch

Teacher Tip
For smaller groups, this game can be adapted to play similar to charades.

Low Intensity:

Practice Makes Heroes

Object

Heroes reinforce the Hero Code while exploring scenarios in which they can show courage.

Preparation

Make sure the recreation area is safe and ready for play. On note cards, write out scenarios of helping others even when it would be difficult to do so for the Heroes to role-play, like playing with the kid on the playground no one else wants to play with, leaving a conversation in which someone is saying unkind things about someone else, donating money they've been saving for a special toy to a worthy cause instead.

Let's Play!

In our second Bible story, our heroes helped people who needed help even when it was hard for them to help. We're going to follow their examples with a role-playing game where we practice helping in difficult situations.

1. Divide the Heroes into small groups (3–5 children each).

2. Give each team a scenario on a notecard, or tell them to come up with a scenario in which they could help someone even when it is difficult to do so.

3. Set a timer for five minutes to let the teams plan their scenes.

4. Have the teams share their scenarios by acting them out for the group. If time and interest permit, they may act out more than one.

Bible Tie-in

Do you think it's difficult to help others when it means doing something that is not easy for you? Why or why not?

What can we do to practice helping others when it's hard for us to help?

It can be difficult to help in situations that are scary or that cause us to give up something we want so that someone else can have what they need. Yet, when we help in these situations, we never know how much our efforts to help can grow down the line.

Women like Shiphrah and Puah helped make sure the Hebrew boys were safe and able to bring happiness to their families. Miriam helped make sure that Moses grew up safe and protected so that he could go on to become a great leader and one of God's heroes. You never know how much good a little help can do!

Preschool Recreation

Help Baby Moses

Preparation

Make sure the recreation area is safe and ready for play.

Let's Play!

SAY: **Miriam was God's helper. She watched over Moses to keep him safe.**

1. Have the Heroes sit on the floor.
2. Choose a child to pretend to be Miriam. Have Miriam go outside of the room with another teacher. Or have Miriam cover their eyes.
3. Hide the baby doll somewhere in the room.
4. Have Miriam come back in the room or uncover their eyes.
5. Let Miriam look for the baby doll. Have the remaining children shout "Hot!" when Miriam is moving close to the doll. Have the remaining children shout "Cold!" when Miriam is moving away from the doll.
6. When Miriam finds the doll have all the children shout, "Heroes are called to help others!"
7. Repeat the game until everyone has an opportunity to be Miriam.

Bible Tie-in

When you are finished, congratulate the children on being such good Heroes.

SAY: **Heroes are called to help others.**

It's Time to Help

Preparation

Make sure the recreation area is safe and ready for play.

Let's Play!

1. Have the children move to an open area of the room.
2. Start the game with you or another leader as the Hero. Have the Hero stand on one side of the room, facing the other side of the room.
3. Have the rest of the children stand on the opposite side of the room, facing the Hero.

SAY: **Let's play a game called "It's Time to Help." All of you except the Hero will say together, "What time is it, Hero?" The Hero will say a time like "It's two o'clock." You will each move two steps forward. Then you will ask the question again. The Hero will tell you another time and you will move forward that many steps. If the Hero says, "It's time to help!" you must turn around and run back to your side of the room. The Hero will chase you and try to tag you.**

Tip: Help the children play the game once so that they understand the rules. If you have older children, let the children take turns being the hero.

Bible Tie-in

SAY: **In our Bible story today, some women were God's helpers. They helped keep baby Moses safe.**

Bible Story

Shiphrah, Puah, and Miriam: God's Wonder Women
Exodus 1:8–2:10

Hotline Verse

So let's strive for the things that bring peace and the things that build each other up.
(Romans 14:19)

Hotline Tip

Heroes are called to…
Help Others!

Materials

Help Baby Moses

- baby doll

Bible Story
Jethro Mentors Moses
Exodus 18

Hotline Verse
So let's strive for the things that bring peace and the things that build each other up.
(Romans 14:19)

Hotline Tip
Heroes are called to... Work Together!

High Intensity:
Work Together Tag

Object
Heroes will reinforce the Hotline Tip while playing a hero-themed game of tag.

Preparation
Make sure the recreation area is safe and ready for play.

Let's Play!
When Moses was leading the Israelites, Jethro advised him to find some other leaders to help him lead the people. Moses listened to Jethro's advice and found a team of leaders to help him. We are going to play a teamwork game similar to the one you know as "Tag" so that we can practice working with others.

1. Select a Hero to be "It."
2. "It" turns their back to the group and covers their face with both hands.
3. Heroes work as a team to select someone who will touch "It." Then the Heroes begin walking around "It" in a circle.
4. When the selected Hero is ready, he or she gently touches "It" on top of the head.
5. "It" must then quickly turn around to see who touched them. All Heroes shake their heads and say, "It wasn't this Hero!"
6. Once "It" guesses the correct Hero, these two Heroes join forces and become "It" together.
7. Repeat as time allows. Those doing the tagging will continue to work together to decide who will tag one of the "It" players. Those playing the role of "It" will work together to figure out who tagged them.

Bible Tie-in
What was the most challenging thing about our game?

How did having teammates to work with help you in this game?

Having people to help us usually makes things easier. We can practice teamwork by making sure to ask for help when we find ourselves in situations where doing things alone would be overwhelming.

Medium Intensity:

Find the Team

Object

Heroes will reinforce the Bible story while playing a teamwork game.

Preparation

Make sure the recreation area is safe and ready for play. Gather supplies and prepare the pieces of paper with the parts of the Bible verse.

Let's Play!

Jethro advised Moses to find a team to help him lead the Israelites. Let's play a game to help us find a team!

1. Give each Hero a slip of paper with one of the three parts of the Hotline Verse written on it. (Make sure the slips of paper are mixed up.)

2. Have the Heroes form a circle, and choose a person to start the game. Without letting anyone else see their paper, that person will call out a random word that is underlined from their portion of the Hotline Verse. If someone else in the circle recognizes the word called out as part of the Hotline Verse that they don't have, they should go and stand to the left of the person who called out the word, becoming part of their team.

3. The person standing to the right of the person who called out the first word will then have a chance to call out a word from their portion of the Hotline Verse and repeat the process of finding a team member.

4. If a player mistakenly tries to form or join a team with a person who has the same part of the Hotline Verse, that player must go back to the circle and wait for another turn after everyone to the right has had a turn. (All who remain in the circle will get more chances to call out words from the verse.)

5. The goal is to form a complete team by finding all three parts of the Hotline Verse. Once a team has all three parts of the verse, the team exits the circle and sits down together.

6. Play until everyone has a team of three representing the complete Hotline Verse.

Bible Tie-in

We had to pay careful attention to the words of the Hotline Verse to make sure that we found all the team members that we needed. I'm sure Moses had to pay careful attention to the people in his community to find the right leaders for his team as well.

What are some other ways that we can make sure that we seek out good helpers or teammates when we need help in our lives?

Let's say our Hero Hotline Verse together one more time: So let's strive for the things that bring peace and the things that build each other up. Romans 14:19

Bible Story

Jethro Mentors Moses
Exodus 18

Hotline Verse

So let's strive for the things that bring peace and the things that build each other up. (Romans 14:19)

Hotline Tip

Heroes are called to… Work Together!

Materials

- slips of paper with parts of the Hotline Verse written on them. Break the verse after the words *strive* and *peace* to form three parts. Underline all the words except *the*, *things*, and *that*.

Optional: whistle

Teacher Tips

- If you anticipate a smaller group, break the verse into two parts. For larger groups, break the verse into more than three parts.
- Add energy by increasing the speed of play. Use a whistle as a signal to speed up the game.

Bible Story

Jethro Mentors Moses
Exodus 18

Hotline Verse

So let's strive for the things that bring peace and the things that build each other up. (Romans 14:19)

Hotline Tip

Heroes are called to... Work Together!

Low Intensity:

Quickening Questions

Object

Heroes will reinforce the Hotline Tip while playing a guessing game similar to Twenty Questions.

Preparation

Make sure the recreation area is safe and ready for play.

Let's Play!

In our Bible story, Moses found leaders to help him lead the Israelite community. He did this because Jethro reminded him that we can accomplish more when we work together.

1. Divide the Heroes into two teams. If you have a large group (twenty or more), consider dividing the group in half and assigning an adult to each group. The adult in each group can then create two teams. If you have mixed ages, pair younger children with older children and encourage them to work together.
2. Explain: **We are going to play a question game. I will think of a real-life thing (like a bicycle, a Bible, a rabbit, a shoe, whatever), and each team will get to ask a question to help guess what it is.**
3. Ask the teams to take turns asking one question each to try and figure out what the mystery object is. Allow them to consult with one another and come to an agreement on their question before asking it. If necessary, clarify that they can't ask directly what the object is.
4. Once they've figured out what the object is, the leader picks another object. If they struggle with identifying the item, the leader can reveal the item and then select a new item.
5. Repeat as many times as there is energy and interest for it.

Bible Tie-in

What kinds of questions do you think were the most helpful in guessing the correct answer?

Was it ever hard to think of a good question? Did you get better at asking questions as the game went along?

If you could ask any question about God or Jesus, what would you ask?

Asking questions to gain understanding is an important part of working together.

Preschool Recreation

Work Together

Preparation

Make sure the recreation area is safe and ready for play.

Let's Play!

Say: **Heroes are called to work together. Let's work together to play a game.**

1. Have the Heroes stand on one side of the room.

2. Give instructions such as the following:

Hero (Child 1), **hold Hero** (Child 2)**'s hand and skip together across the room.**

Hero (Child 1), **hold Hero** (Child 2)**'s hand and gallop together across the room.**

Hero (Child 1), **hold Hero** (Child 2)**'s hand and hop together around the table one time.**

Hero (Child 1), **hold Hero** (Child 2)**'s hand and sit down together on the same chair.**

Hero (Child 1), **hold Hero** (Child 2)**'s hand and tiptoe together across the room.**

Hero (Child 1), **hold Hero** (Child 2)**'s hand and walk backward together across the room.**

Bible Tie-in

When you are finished, congratulate the children on being such good Heroes.

SAY: **Heroes are called to work together.**

Moses Tag

Preparation

Make sure the recreation area is safe and ready for play.

Let's Play!

SAY: **Moses chose other people to be leaders.**

1. Have the Heroes move to an open area of the room.

2. Choose one child to be Moses.

3. Have the rest of the children move around the room. Have Moses try to tag a child. When a child is tagged, have the child hold hands with Moses. The tagged child has become one of Moses's leaders. Now Moses and the leader work together to try to tag another child and make a group of three.

4. After there is a group of three, choose a different Moses and play the game again.

TIP: Help the Heroes play the game once so that they understand the rules. Play the game until each child has an opportunity to be Moses.

Bible Tie-in

SAY: **In our Bible story today, Moses chose other people to work together with him to lead the people.**

SAY: **Heroes are called to work together.**

Bible Story

Jethro Mentors Moses
Exodus 18

Hotline Verse

So let's strive for the things that bring peace and the things that build each other up.
(Romans 14:19)

Hotline Tip

Heroes are called to…
Work Together!

Bible Story
The Magnificent Magi
Matthew 2:1-12

Hotline Verse
So let's strive for the things that bring peace and the things that build each other up.
(Romans 14:19)

Hotline Tip
Heroes are called to…
Listen to God!

Materials
- cones or masking tape
- pool noodles or soft bats
- balloons

High Intensity:
Guided by a Star

Object
Heroes work on their listening skills and attention skills.

Preparation
Make sure the recreation area is safe and ready for play. Use cones or masking tape to mark a starting line and a finish line. Blow up three balloons for each team.

Let's Play!
In our Bible story, one of the ways the magi recognized God guiding them was through a star. Today, we're going to play a game in which we will be guided by listening for the word *star*.

We are going to work together to win a race by listening and paying attention. Each team will work together to get three "gifts" (balloons) from "The East" to Jerusalem. You must move one balloon at a time using the pool noodles (or soft bats). If the balloon touches the ground or one of the players, the team must return to the starting line and begin again. While you're traveling, I'll be saying words from our story. Anytime you hear the word *star* you must stop moving your feet, but you can catch and hold the balloon until I say another word. Any team who moves after I say the word *star* must return to the starting line and begin again. The first team to get all three gifts to Jerusalem wins.

1. Divide Heroes into teams of three. Have them line up together at the starting line.

2. On your signal, the team begins bouncing a balloon in the air with the pool noodles, moving it toward the finish line.

3. While Heroes play, say random words from the Bible story. Sprinkle in a number of words that begin with *s*.

4. Repeat if time and interest allow.

Bible Tie-in
Was it hard to pay attention and listen for the word *star* while you were moving across the room? Why or why not? What about when your teammates were calling out to you in the game? Why or why not?

The magi had to pay attention to God's leading while they were on the move as well. This probably made their journey challenging also.

Distractions in our daily lives also make it harder to listen for and look for God's leading in our lives.

What are some ways that we can better focus on listening for God's leading in our own lives?

Medium Intensity:

Return Home Another Way

Object

Heroes work together to "return home another way."

Preparation

Make sure the recreation area is clear and safe for play. Use cones or masking tape to mark a starting line and a finish line.

Let's Play!

Once the magi had visited Jesus in Jerusalem, God told them to go back home another way so they wouldn't run into Herod again.

In this game, we're going to work together to move across the play space, returning home. We must move together as a group. We can only step inside the hula hoops, but a hula hoop cannot move if someone is standing inside it.

Optional: If you play this game after "Guided by a Star" (p. 18), have the Heroes move in the opposite direction you established there to emulate returning home.

1. Start a timer to time how long it takes the group to move from the starting line to the finish line.

2. The first person will lay the hula hoop on the ground. Two to three more people will then get into the hula hoop with the first person.

3. Those still behind the starting line will hand another hula hoop to those in the first hula hoop, who will lay the second hula hoop down next to the first. They will then move from the first to the second hula hoop, making room for more Heroes to move into the first one.

4. Play continues with Heroes passing hula hoops down the row to make space to move forward. Once all Heroes are inside hula hoops, they must pass one extra hula hoop down the row to allow everyone to move forward, then pick up the last hula hoop they just exited and pass it down to continue moving forward.

5. Repeat if time and interest allow to see if Heroes can beat their previous time.

Bible Tie-in

What made moving difficult? What made moving easier? What kinds of things did you have to say to one another in order to move quickly and safely? What and who did you have to listen to in order to know what to do next? How did you help your fellow teammates?

Sometimes listening for God's voice means that we have to really focus and pay attention. Having people to help you hear what God has to say can make it easier to hear God.

What are some ways that the church can work together to listen for and hear God?

Bible Story

The Magnificent Magi
Matthew 2:1-12

Hotline Verse

So let's strive for the things that bring peace and the things that build each other up.
(Romans 14:19)

Hotline Tip

Heroes are called to…
Listen to God!

Materials

- hula hoops, one for about every four Heroes
- cones
- masking tape
- stopwatch

Bible Story
The Magnificent Magi
Matthew 2:1-12

Hotline Verse
So let's strive for the things that bring peace and the things that build each other up.
(Romans 14:19)

Hotline Tip
Heroes are called to…
Listen to God!

Materials
- coin

Low Intensity:
Heroic Attention

Object
Heroes will reinforce the Hotline Tip while playing a teamwork sleight of hand game.

Preparation
Make sure the recreation area is safe and ready for play. Arrange tables end to end with enough seating space for the group.

Let's Play!
In our Bible story, the magi pay close attention to signs of God's guiding. Let's practice listening and paying attention to guiding.

1. Divide the group into two teams and choose a captain for each team. (If your group is very large, you can divide into more teams and play round-robin style.)
2. Ask teams to sit on opposite sides of the table.
3. Give the captain of Team 1 a coin. On your signal, players from Team 1 pass the coin from hand to hand under the table.
4. Whenever the captain of Team 2 is ready, they will shout, "Heroes are called to listen to God!" All members of Team 1 must then raise their fists in the air.
5. The captain of Team 2 shouts, "So let's strive for the things that bring peace and the things that build each other up!" At that point, all members of Team 1 place their hands flat on the table. The player with the coin must be careful not to give away its location to the opposing team.
6. Through listening and observation, Team 2 has two guesses to determine as a group who has the coin. The person they guess must pick up both hands, revealing whether or not they have the coin.
7. Play again after giving the coin to Team 2. Continue to play as long as there is time and interest.

Bible Tie-in
God's heroes pay attention to the little signs of God's presence around them. In our game, we listened for the cues to do certain things. We also paid attention to the behavior of others around us so that we could work together to find out where the coin was. It can also be helpful for us to work together to look for God's guidance in our lives.

Can you think of any situations where you had to listen or pay attention to find God's guidance?

Preschool Recreation

Listen!

Preparation

Make sure the recreation area is safe and ready for play.

Let's Play!

SAY: **Heroes are called to listen to God. Let's play a game like Simon Says. We'll call it Hero Says. When you hear me say "Hero Says" do whatever motion I tell you to do. But listen carefully. If I do not say "Hero Says," do not do the motion.**

1. Play this game like "Simon Says." You or another Sidekick will be the Hero.
2. Have the children line up facing the Hero.
3. The Hero calls out a number of motions by first saying "Hero Says…" (hop, jump, run in place, and so forth.) The children must then perform that motion.
4. Anytime the Hero calls out a motion without saying "Hero Says…" the children should *not* do it. If anyone does, do not make them stop the game. Just say, "Uh oh! I did not say 'Hero Says.'" And then continue with all the children.

Bible Tie-in

SAY: **The wise men listened to God. Heroes are called to listen to God.**

Walk Like a Camel

Preparation

Make sure the recreation area is safe and ready for play.

Let's Play!

SAY: **Sometimes we see pictures of the wise men riding camels. Let's pretend to be camels.**

1. Show the Heroes how to bend slightly at the waist and to do a bumpy/jerky kind of walk such as a camel would do in the sand.
2. Have the Heroes practice camel walking.
3. Explain that the children are part of a camel caravan, a group of camels crossing the desert. Everyone must follow single file.
4. Hold up the star sign and let the children pretend to be camels as they follow you all around the room and out into the hall.

Bible Tie-in

SAY: **In our Bible story, the wise men followed a bright star to find the new king.**

Bible Story

The Magnificent Magi
Matthew 2:1-12

Hotline Verse

So let's strive for the things that bring peace and the things that build each other up.
(Romans 14:19)

Hotline Tip

Heroes are called to…
Listen to God!

Materials Walk Like a Camel

- one of the star signs from the **Hero Hotline Preschool/ Kindergarten Leader** pages 86-87

Bible Story
Unexpected Heroes Give Paul a Basket Ride
Acts 9:1-25

Hotline Verse
So let's strive for the things that bring peace and the things that build each other up.
(Romans 14:19)

Hotline Tip
Heroes are called to… Show Grace!

Materials
- pool noodles cut to one foot in length, one for each child

High Intensity:
Grace Tag

Object
Heroes reinforce the Hotline Tip while playing a modified game of tag.

Preparation
Make sure the recreation area is safe and ready for play. Gather the pool noodles together near the play area. (If your play area is small, you may wish to cut the pool noodles down to a smaller size so kids will have to get closer to tag each other.)

Let's Play!
Let's all repeat our Hotline Tip together. *(Say the Tip in unison.)* **Heroes are called to Show Grace!**

Explain: **At Damascus, the disciples showed grace to Paul. Even though they were unsure of Paul, they helped him and welcomed him into their community. Showing grace is when you offer acceptance or inclusion to someone, even when we're not sure they deserve to be included. We're going to play a game where we show grace too… with pool noodles!**

1. Gather the Heroes together. Pick someone to be "It."
2. On your signal, the game will begin and "It" will use a pool noodle to (gently) tag other kids. When tagging someone, "It" says the Hotline Tip, "Heroes are called to Show Grace."
3. Once children are tagged, they grab a pool noodle and join "It" to tag people too. Remind them always to say "Heroes are called to Show Grace" every time they tag someone.
4. Last one to be tagged is the new "It." Play again as many times as desired.

Bible Tie-in
The disciples in Damascus accepted Paul into their community because as followers of Jesus, they were called to show grace to everyone, even someone who was previously unkind to them. In helping Paul, they accepted him into their community. In the game we played, instead of a tagged person being "out," we showed grace by including them in the community.

As followers of Jesus, we must show grace even when it's hard or we don't feel like it.

Can you think of a time that you showed grace in a situation where you didn't particularly want to show grace? How did you feel afterward?

Medium Intensity:

Team Up!

Object

Kids will use a parachute to practice teamwork.

Preparation

Make sure the recreation area is safe and ready for play. Arrange the parachute in the middle of the space. Place the beach ball(s) nearby.

Let's Play!

Explain: **In our Bible story, the disciples in Damascus worked together to help Paul by saving him from those who wanted to hurt him. Let's play a game in which we practice working together as a team.**

1. Gather the Heroes in a circle around the parachute. Put one beach ball in the middle of the parachute. Ask one child to pick up the edge of the parachute. Ask her or him to try to toss the beach ball into the air using the parachute.

Optional: You can let each child have a turn to try this.

2. Now ask all the Heroes to grab the edge of the parachute with both hands. Have them wave the parachute randomly (this should make the ball move and bounce a little).

3. Have the Heroes all lower the parachute to the floor at one time, then quickly raise it in unison to bounce the ball. (This may take a little while to coordinate. Keep having them try until they are successful.)

4. Challenge the Heroes to see how high they can get the ball and still keep it on the parachute.

5. Challenge them to move the ball from one side of the parachute to another by having different Heroes on each side move the parachute to move the ball back and forth.

6. Have the Heroes walk the parachute around the play space while still bouncing the ball.

Additional Challenges (if time permits): Repeat any of the previous steps with more than one ball. If your parachute has a hole or circle in the middle, pretend the ball is "Paul," and try to get the ball into the middle. (Remind the children that the disciples in Damascus helped Paul escape through a hole in the wall of the city.) They can also try rolling it around the outside edge of the parachute.

Bible Tie-in

Why do you think we were able to bounce the ball better when we all lifted the parachute together? *(Teamwork/unified motion was stronger.)*

When we work together, it is easier to do things that show grace to others like the disciples in our Bible story who worked together to help Paul.

One person alone can do good things, but together we can accomplish many great things.

Bible Story

Unexpected Heroes Give Paul a Basket Ride
Acts 9:1-25

Hotline Verse

So let's strive for the things that bring peace and the things that build each other up.
(Romans 14:19)

Hotline Tip

Heroes are called to… Show Grace!

Materials

- large play parachute *(If you don't have access to a parachute, a large flat bedsheet can substitute.)*
- one or more inflated beach balls

Bible Story
Unexpected Heroes Give Paul a Basket Ride
Acts 9:1-25

Hotline Verse
So let's strive for the things that bring peace and the things that build each other up.
(Romans 14:19)

Hotline Tip
Heroes are called to... Show Grace!

Materials
(a variety for each team)
- construction paper
- children's scissors
- ribbon
- tape
- craft sticks
- other craft supplies of your choosing
- action figure (one per team)

Low Intensity:
Build a Basket

Object
Heroes will reinforce the Bible story and their teamwork skills and Hotline Tip.

Preparation
Make sure the recreation area is safe and ready for play. Set up a table at one end of the room representing "the city wall." Gather the necessary supplies for the activity and arrange in piles for each team.

Let's Play!
In our Bible story, the disciples in Damascus helped Paul escape his enemies by lowering him in a basket through a hole in the city wall. Let's play a game to help us remember the Bible story.

1. Explain: **The disciples had to find a basket suitable for lowering Paul to safety. Can you imagine a basket big enough and sturdy enough for that? The disciples probably had to work quickly and quietly to avoid being caught by those who wanted to harm Paul. Let's build our own baskets to quickly and quietly lower Paul over our wall.**

2. Divide the Heroes into teams. Explain to the children that the table you set up represents the city wall.

3. Give each team their pile of assorted materials and action figure.

4. Instruct the teams to build a basket that they think will hold for lowering the action figure representing Paul. Challenge them to work quietly as the disciples in Damascus must have.

5. Once each team has built their basket, they should move quickly together to the other side of the room, put the Paul figurine in the basket and, leaning over the table, attempt to lower Paul down to the ground on the other side of the table.

6. The teams whose baskets hold will be considered winners.

Optional: Have a show-and-tell of the baskets that survived the wall. Award a first, second, and third place for the most creative basket design.

Bible Tie-in
Let's all say today's Hotline Tip together! Heroes are called to Show Grace!

Can you imagine putting a real man in a basket and lowering him by hand through a high city wall? The disciples must have worked hard together to accomplish that and to make sure that Paul was safe.

When we work together, we can do amazing things!